# WARTIME CAMDEN

CONTENTS

ISBN 0 901389 40 4

# FOR KING AND COUNTRY

When war was declared on 4 August 1914, every attempt was made by the Government to encourage men to join the forces.

G. R.

## Your King & Country Need You.

### Another 100,000 Men Wanted

Lord Kitchener is much gratified with the response already made to the Appeal for additional men for His Majesty's Regular Army.

In the grave National emergency that now confronts the Empire he asks with renewed confidence that another 100,000 men will now come forward.

#### TERMS OF SERVICE:
(Extension of Age Limit.)
Age on enlistment **19** to **35**, Ex-Soldiers up to **45**, and certain selected Ex-Non-Commissioned Officers up to **50**. Height 5ft. 3in. and upwards. Chest **34** inches at least. Must be medically fit.

General Service for the War.

Men enlisting for the duration of the War will be able to claim discharge, with all convenient speed, at the conclusion of the War.

#### PAY AT ARMY RATES,
and Married Men or Widowers with Children will be accepted, and will draw Separation Allowance under Army conditions.

#### HOW TO JOIN.
Men wishing to join should apply in person at any Military Barrack or at any Recruiting Office : the address of the latter can be obtained from Post Offices or Labour Exchanges.

### GOD SAVE THE KING.

**1** Recruiting advertisement which appeared in the **Hampstead and Highgate Express** of 5 September 1914

However, even before the outbreak of war, there were several volunteer corps already in existence.

One of these was the "Artists Rifles", 28th Battalion London Regiment (Artists Rifles). Founded in 1860 as the 38th Middlesex (Artists) Rifle Volunteers, this was one of the volunteer corps converted into the Territorial force under Lord Haldane's army reorganisation of 1907.

As early as 1910, due to a far-sighted commanding officer, a plan of action in the event of mobilization had been prepared. This involved the commandeering of a hotel and schools for barracks and accommodation and stabling for their horses.

The Rifles were one of many units who found Hampstead Heath an ideal training ground. Also, as the following passage illustrates, the natives were decidedly friendly!

'Although I had at the time I write of only the vaguest notion of what work was likely to be required of the Battalion before the war ended, I could not help feeling that our "London duties" were only temporary, and as I much desired to keep my men "fit" and "hard", in preparation for whatever might thereafter be required of them, I sent each day all men not engaged in other special duties for a "route march" to Hampstead, for a good hard day's work there (in accordance with a specially prepared programme). It thus came about that every morning about 10 o'clock a contingent of "Artists", on their way to Hampstead, would march up Fitzjohn's Avenue under one of my Majors, and this, being a broad commodious thoroughfare, they got into the habit of having their first "halt" there. The effect of this was that the inhabitants there came to know us and look for us, and when we halted there (so I was told, I was never in charge of the Hampstead contingent myself!), masses of young ladies (and a few older ones – God bless them!) used to appear with cake, sandwiches, wine, coffee, tea, cyder, etc., and got to know the names of some of the men, and to attach themselves to the various Companies, and the halt became more like a summer garden party than a war-time halt – for at that time all soldiers, even amateurs like ourselves, were very popular in this country! Hearing of this, I thought that it might be better *not* to halt at exactly the same place each day – it looked like *asking* for hospitality – so one day, at my suggestion, the Major in command continued his march without halting there, to the intense mortification of the hospitable inhabitants who had the meal prepared as usual. I received so many really kindly-meant protests that my heart melted. I waived my objection, and the daily entertainment was continued so long as we remained in London!'
**MAY, Colonel H.A.R. Memories of the Artists Rifles. Howlett & Son, 1929, p 131**

Even **The Times** noted that big boys were now playing at soldiers on the Heath, and commented that 'for all their set faces and stalwart bodies they seem still pitifully young, these big children of England'.
**The Times,** 10 March 1915, p 13

**2** Artists Rifles sentry on the Lancing Street Schools. Lancing Street and Manchester Street Schools were commandeered on 5 August 1914. They became barracks and sleeping accommodation for the men

**3** The Artists Rifles corps had its headquarters at Duke's Road, St. Pancras.

**4** Royal Engineers Signal Service in training on Hampstead Heath – an advance lookout party, January 1915

However, not everybody contemplated war with enthusiasm; James Albert Reeks, for one, as his daughter relates:

'My father aged 36 years lost his job and was told by his employer to join the army. He tried to get work, without success. The reply from prospective employers was "A young man like you should be in the army". So my father unwillingly joined the Army Service Corps leaving behind five children and a pregnant wife.
I remember his parcel of clothing arriving containing his only decent suit and his pair of boots, wrapped in the jacket and tied with his bootlaces, on which was a luggage label. The suit was brushed and put away to await his return.'
**Sarah Reeks**

James Albert Reeks never returned to civilian life. He survived the war, but died of pneumonia in March 1919, before his demobilization.

Others succumbed to disease during the war. William Carson, a private in the 2nd London Regiment, sent a postcard dated 17 August 1917 to his family in Cotleigh Road, Kilburn, telling them that he was a prisoner of war in Germany. A few months later, they received news that he had died of intestinal catarrh while a prisoner.

Even of those who survived few can have been unmarked, either physically or psychologically, by their experiences. Albert Edward Elsy, chief photographer and later managing director of the Langfier Studio, 343 Finchley Road, NW3, was invalided home from the front line in France suffering from shell shock.

Hugh Turpin speaks of the telegraph boys, messengers of doom, whose arrival was universally dreaded:

'Often seen in Hampstead, during W.W.I. were telegraph boys, riding bicycles, and wearing their distinctive caps, who were busy delivering telegrams, informing the wives and relatives of men at the front, that their men folk were killed, or missing in action. People dreaded seeing these boys cycling down their road, and they fearfully peeped through their windows, hoping that the boy would not knock on their front door, and hand them the fateful telegram.'
**Hugh Turpin**

Two of the most poignant items in the Local History Library's collection were found among the effects of a lady who died in Kentish Town in 1978. They were the official Army notification of the death of her husband, Gunner Edwin Prosser, and the letter of sympathy from the nurse who had been with him when he died.

**5** Men of the Queen Victoria Rifles, 9th London Regiment seen during training near Whitestone Pond, Hampstead, January 1915

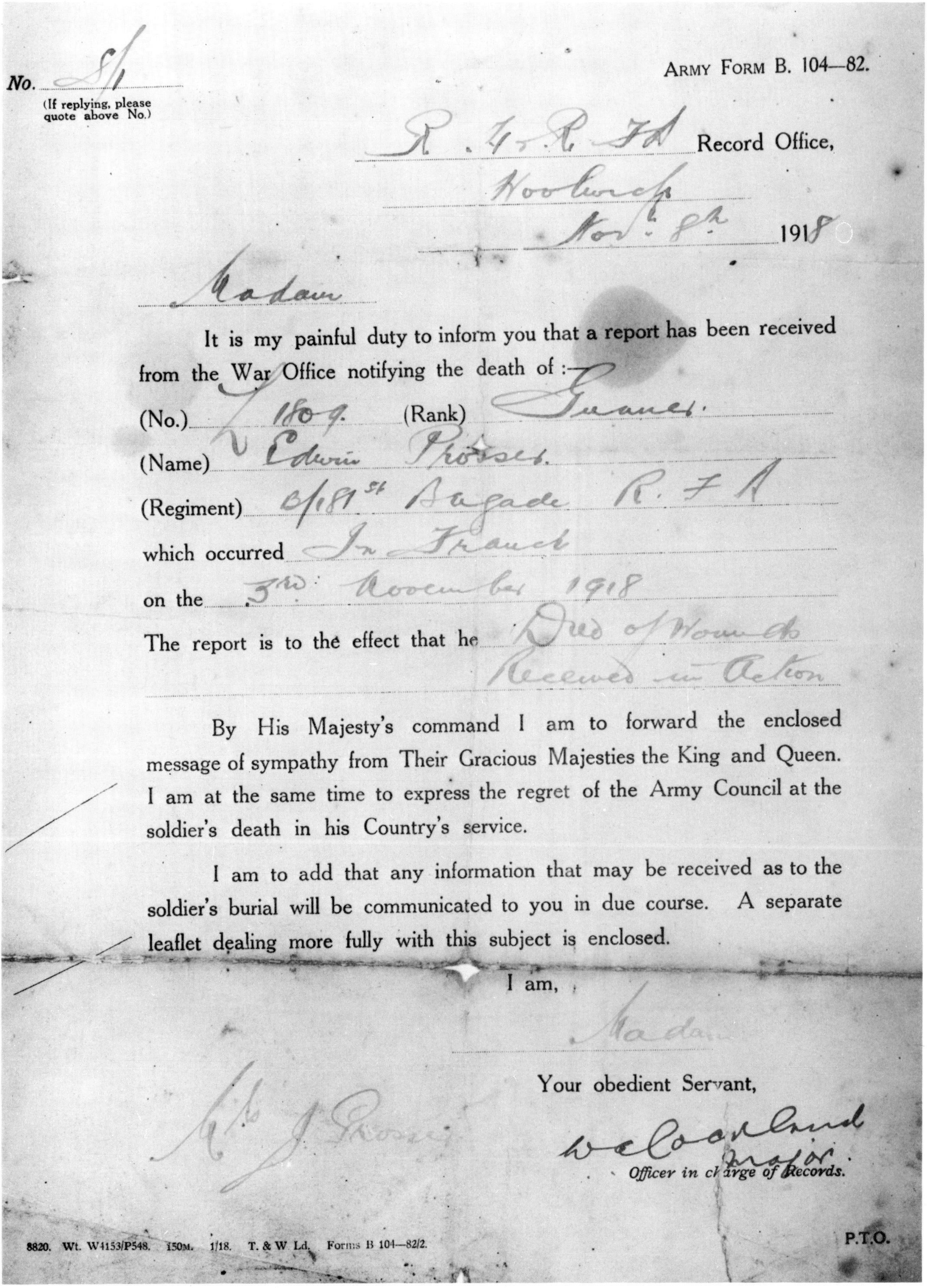

No. 8/1

(If replying, please quote above No.)

ARMY FORM B. 104—82.

R. G. A. F. A. Record Office,

Woolwich

Nov: 8th 1918

Madam

It is my painful duty to inform you that a report has been received from the War Office notifying the death of :—

(No.) L/1809. (Rank) Gunner.

(Name) Edwin Prosser.

(Regiment) C/181st Brigade R. F. A

which occurred In France

on the 3rd November 1918

The report is to the effect that he Died of Wounds Received in Action

By His Majesty's command I am to forward the enclosed message of sympathy from Their Gracious Majesties the King and Queen. I am at the same time to express the regret of the Army Council at the soldier's death in his Country's service.

I am to add that any information that may be received as to the soldier's burial will be communicated to you in due course. A separate leaflet dealing more fully with this subject is enclosed.

I am,

Madam

Your obedient Servant,

Mrs J. Prosser

W. E. Cockland Major

*Officer in charge of Records.*

8820. Wt. W4153/P548. 150M. 1/18. T. & W Ld. Forms B 104—82/2.

P.T.O.

**6** Official letter notifying his wife of the death of Gunner Edwin Prosser of wounds received in action, November 1918

# CHAPTER TWO

# HELPING OUR WOUNDED

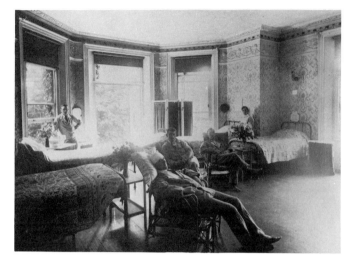

**8** Patients in one of the wards at Rosslyn Lodge Auxiliary Hospital, Lyndhurst Road, Hampstead

Hugh Turpin remembers women pinning white feathers on any man who looked as if he should be at the front:

'A young man I knew who early on in the war, had lost an arm in Flanders, had a white feather pinned on him. Evidently the lady did not notice his loss of arm. He thanked her, smiled, and walked on.'
**Hugh Turpin**

For men like this wounded at the front, extra hospital facilities and beds were desperately needed. Hampstead and Highgate, with many large houses, seemed admirably fitted for this purpose. Unfortunately, such houses were often damp, draughty and without proper drainage, making them highly unsuitable for the wounded; for example, "Cedar Lawn" in North End Road had been on the verge of being pulled down when its owner, Sir William Lever offered it to the Hampstead Red Cross V.A.D. (Voluntary Aid Detachment).

**7** Rosslyn Lodge Auxiliary Hospital, Lyndhurst Road, Hampstead

**9** The Artists Rifles V.A.D. Hospital, Lyndhurst Road, Hampstead

**10** Artists Rifles V.A.D. Hospital. Patients knitting

Rosslyn Lodge in Lyndhurst Road also became an Auxiliary Hospital. It had been put at the disposal of the V.A.D. by its owner, Mr. Hill and was opened as a hospital in the summer of 1916. Money for equipment and for making the house fit to receive the soldiers had been raised by appeals and a flag day. Kenwood House also underwent a new lease of life:

**'During the war my mother (Matilda Annie Turpin) nursed wounded soldiers in Kenwood House on Hampstead Heath, given as a war hospital by the Grand Duke Michael Michaelovitch, cousin of Nicholas the Second of Russia. She was awarded a silver decoration by the Grand Duke. This decoration of a distinctly Russian character, is inscribed on the back, "To those who serve, without need of recognition or hope of reward, from the American Hospital".' ".'**
**Hugh Turpin**

The poet Robert Graves was one of those wounded in action. He was taken to Queen Alexandra's Hospital in Highgate, opened in March 1915 in Brookfield House, Millfield Lane. Here, Graves enjoyed the luxury of a private room, as he relates in his autobiography "Goodbye To All That".
Another private house pressed into service as a military hospital was 4 Lyndhurst Road, Hampstead, which became the Artists Rifles V.A.D. Hospital.

Another institution involved in helping the wounded was the Hampstead War Hospital Supply Depot opened at 91 Finchley Road on 19 July 1915. The **HAMPSTEAD AND HIGHGATE EXPRESS** of 10 July 1915, invited the ladies of Hampstead to support this depot by coming forward to "work voluntarily in the manufacture of articles actually needed for the management of the large war hospitals established in the Dardanelles, in Egypt, Belgium, Serbia, France and elsewhere. Every article will be made to an approved pattern, and sent off direct to the hospitals."

The expenses of equipping and running the depot were met from the weekly subscriptions of its workers and the generous public response to an appeal from the Mayor of Hampstead. All labour was voluntary.

**"SPARE WHAT YOU CAN FOR OTHER MEN LIKE ME,"** and send to The Hampstead War Hospital Supply Depot, **91** Finchley Road, who have hundreds working for the wounded but **URGENTLY WANT MONEY** to buy materials. **EVERY SHILLING YOU GIVE** BUYS something a Wounded Man needs.

**11** Advertisement for the Hampstead War Hospital Supply Depot, which appeared in the **Hampstead and Highgate Express** of 7 April 1917

**12** War Hospital Supply Depot staff engaged in producing hospital supplies. Items made here included roller bandages, bed jackets, towels, splints, crutches, pyjamas and swabs

# CHAPTER THREE

# "ONLY SOLDIERS GET KILLED"

For the first time warfare was brought to the civilian's doorstep. The feelings of Albert Moody, on seeing a bombed-out house in Gospel Oak, probably sum up those of many people:—

**'This was terrible – what an outrage, killing civilians like this, only soldiers get killed in wartime.'**
**Albert Moody**

It is difficult to discover exactly where the bombs fell in Camden, as censorship and the need to keep morale high prevented any detailed reporting of such incidents in the local newspapers.

The accompanying table, although probably incomplete, does give some idea of events in Camden. This information was collated from two main sources: an article compiled from the records of the London Fire Brigade and found in a cuttings scrapbook in the Guildhall Library, and two manuscript volumes compiled by Arthur H. Bird and entitled "The London Air Raids" in the Imperial War Museum.

At first, Zeppelin raids had a novelty value. People were more interested in the marauders than in the idea of taking cover. Gradually, however, with increasing raids and the superseding of Zeppelins by aeroplanes, sheltering became a way of life.

The Government encouraged people to stay in their homes during raids, and many were happy to do so:—

**'The first air raid I recall experiencing was on a Sunday morning, I believe. We all huddled under the stairs in the hall with cups of tea and slices of bread pudding from a baking tin.'**
**John Walter**

Others found it expedient to seek refuge elsewhere:—

**'One particular evening, the Zeppelins were over as usual, and we, with other families, made our way to a fishmongers shop (John Gow)\* where we sheltered in the cellar.'**
**Hugh Turpin**

The vaulted cellars of the Flask Tavern, Hampstead, were also used as air raid shelters. During one raid (possibly that of December 1917) Louise Eickhoff distinctly remembers how she and her sister (the family lived at 14 Gardnor Road) were rushed into this shelter by their babysitter, who was minding them while their mother and grandmother were at the cinema.

\*293 Finchley Road

## World War I    Air Raids in Camden

**8th September 1915**
3 incendiary bombs on Ormond Yard, Holborn.

Bomb outside the National Penny Bank in Theobalds Road. It also broke a gas main in Lambs Conduit Passage, killing one man, injuring sixteen, and damaging a block of buildings including the Dolphin Pub which caught fire.

2 incendiary bombs between Woburn Place and Upper Bedford Place.

1 incendiary bomb in Russell Square.

**13th October 1915**
Gray's Inn and Lincoln's Inn.

The above were raids carried out by Zeppelins, but from now on, all raids on Camden were by aeroplanes, mainly Gothas.

**13th June 1917**
Holborn.

**7th July 1917**
Daylight raid. One man was killed and three injured in St Pancras Road, and great damage caused to the Midland Railway's goods station at Somers Town.

**4th September 1917**
Regent's Park, Haverstock Hill, Kentish Town, Hampstead and Highgate.

**24th September 1917**
112lb. bomb fell at the entrance to Bedford Hotel, Southampton Row. 13 people killed and 26 injured.

**28th September 1917**
Holborn.

**30th September 1917**
Highgate.

**6th December 1917**
Grays Inn Road and Euston Square.

**18th December 1917**
Holborn, Lincolns Inn and Kentish Town, 2 people killed and 7 injured in Wicklow Street, Kings Cross.

**28th January 1918**
Holborn and Kilburn.

**17th February 1918**
Holborn. 20 killed and 22 injured at St Pancras Station.

**7th March 1918**
Hampstead.

**19th May 1918**
Kentish Town and Haverstock Hill.
**This was the last raid of the war on London.**

Compiled from the records of the London Fire Brigade.

## TUBES AND SHELTERS.

On the grounds mentioned at the foot of page 2, the Home Secretary, who is the responsible Minister of the Crown in this matter, concluded his speech to a Conference of Metropolitan Mayors on the 16th October, by saying :

"IT IS GENERALLY DESIRABLE THAT PEOPLE SHOULD "BE ENCOURAGED TO REMAIN IN THEIR OWN HOMES."

If you have to find shelter in a Tube Station coolness and care for others will be necessary for their safety and your own. It is dangerous to leave the platform because of the live rail ; all pushing and crowding should therefore be avoided.

The diseases caused by crowding in the Tubes, the weariness, sleeplessness and excitement of little children, are a greater danger to life than all the guns put together.

The London hospitals hardly felt the air raid casualties ; it was the children's hospitals afterwards that had the work to do.

## IN THE HOUSE.

*Advice from the Chief Commissioner of Police.*

If you are in a building on the top floor, go downstairs where you will have the best available cover overhead, avoiding lift wells, open stairways, and parts of the building under skylights.

Close your doors and do not look out of windows. Keep in a part of a room or passage where you will be out of the line of fragments of metal or *débris* which may enter by a window or door if a bomb should explode outside.

Do not crowd in a basement with only a single means of exit. The fumes from all bombs are injurious if breathed in any quantity, and it is advisable to have a second means of exit in case fumes should enter, or a gas pipe be broken, or rapid escape be necessary for any other reason.

## SAVING THE CHILDREN.

Women with child who dread the sound of the guns near by, and mothers whose children's nerves have been badly shaken, should apply at The Health Institute, Kingsgate Road, or at 27 Heath Street. We may be able to get some away.

Price 2/- per 100 copies.

Not for self but for all.

# THE AIR RAIDS

What to do—and how to do it.

What to be—and how to be it.

*Printed for the Hampstead Council of Social Welfare, at 27 Heath Street, and at the Health Institute, Kingsgate Road.*

B6

**13** Leaflet printed by Hampstead Council of Social Welfare advising people on what to do during an air raid

Tube stations were pressed into service for shelters:–

'After that first air raid, whenever there was an air raid warning, we would run to Warren Street Underground Station for shelter. Once, when descending the winding stairs to the station platforms, I was very frightened when, being small, my windpipe was pushed against the banister.' **John Walter**

None of those Camden residents whose reminiscences we have and who were children during the 1914-18 war appear to have been bombed out of their homes. Others were not so fortunate:–

'I shall never forget London's worst Zeppelin raid for that night of October 13 1915 came very near to being my last in this world – I was one of the Priests of St. Alban's, Holborn and had rooms in Grays Inn Square. Coming back late from the boys' club, I climbed rather wearily up the old oak stairs to my rooms, and sat down in my armchair to take off my boots. I had taken one off when I heard a terrific explosion evidently quite near by. This was the bomb that fell at the top of Chancery Lane. "The Zeppelins are here again", I said to myself. "I'm going to get out of this; downstairs is safer". With one boot on I got as far as the landing. At that moment the next bomb exploded in the garden just beneath my rooms. All I remember is the loudest explosion I ever heard accompanied by a loud incessant singing noise in my ears. Then I saw a great oak door suddenly lift itself off its hinges and fly past me at a great speed just missing my head. There was a noise of falling brickwork and flying glass all round me. A terrific tornado of wind took me off my feet and I found myself flying through the air and then everything seemed suddenly to go out – complete blank and blackness. The next thing I remember was a bright light shining in my eyes and two tall people standing over me talking to one another. I heard one say, "He's dead. I'm afraid to get him out of this". On hearing this I woke up with a start and said, "No, I'm not. I've been blown up by a Zepp. bomb". It was a policeman shining his torch on me. I had been blown by the explosion down two flights of stairs and was lying in the street almost completely buried by fallen brickwork. My clothes were torn to ribbons but I was unhurt except for a deep cut on my left hand and several minor bruises and aches. My rooms were wrecked and the roof simply did not exist any more. The two policemen conducted me to the house of a friend. When he opened the door I said "I have just been blown up by a Zepp. bomb". He said, "Good heavens! Come inside and sit down". I decided after a rest to go to my father's home at Hampstead for the night and borrowed some clothes from my friend. Later, I got into the Tube Station at Chancery Lane for Hampstead.'

(Eye-witness account of the Rev. Philip S. Sidney, curate at St. Alban the Martyr Church, Holborn from 1913-16; from **Arthur H. Bird** (compiler). The London Air Raids. 2 volumes undated.) (Manuscript volumes in the Imperial War Museum).

An incident that lingered in the minds of several Camden residents was the destruction of the Zeppelin at Cuffley, Herts. This airship, which came to a spectacular end on 3 September 1916, was the L21 carrying a crew of 16 and largely wood-built. The aeroplane pilot responsible for her destruction was Lieutenant William Leefe Robinson whose action won him the Victoria Cross.

**14** Air raid damage to the German Gymnasium, Pancras Road,
King's Cross, during a daylight aeroplane raid, 7 July 1917

**17** Damage to the Bedford Hotel, Southampton Row, caused by an aeroplane raid of 24 September 1917. A 50 kilo bomb was dropped opposite the hotel; 13 people were killed and 26 injured

**15** The St. Pancras Hotel, showing the smashed turret in the Hotel Tower and the damaged glass roof of the entrance to the booking hall, after the aeroplane raid of 17/18 February 1918. Six bombs were dropped in rapid succession on or close to St. Pancras Station. 20 people sheltering under the archway beneath the hotel were killed, and 19 injured by flying fragments from these bombs

**16** The result of an air raid on Gray's Inn, 13/14 October 1915

This Zeppelin incident also had a Camden connection:–

'As I looked to the sky, I observed a Zeppelin caught in the rays of the search lights. At times the search lights picked up a single aeroplane flying near the Zeppelin. Very soon tracer bullets could be seen directed at the middle of the envelope of the airship.
Incendiary bullets must have been mingled with the tracer bullets, because very soon, small tongues of fire were licking the side of the Zeppelin. The fire grew with such an intensity, that the very heavens seemed to be on fire.
Pieces of burning material detached themselves from the airship and floated slowly to earth. There was a feeling of a great tragedy being enacted in an awesome, and unhurried manner. Then the frame work of the Zeppelin buckled, and the inferno dropped out of the sky.
...... The wreckage of the Zeppelin came down at Cuffley, just north of London. The bodies of the German crew were transported in a lorry to a garage (converted to a mortuary) at the bottom of the road where I lived (Rosemont Road)* until such time as burial could be arranged. I well remember my mother saying "Poor devils, they are some mother's sons". The wreckage of the Zeppelin was exhibited in a large tent in the central London area (City Road) with admission receipts going to a war charity.'
**Hugh Turpin**

'. . . the muffled gunfire in the distance renewed memories of raids during the Kaiser's war, the burning Zepp; and bodies falling to earth at Cuffley, seen from the Whitestone Pond, the first impression of awe at the sight and then the cheers as it was seen that our brave airman flew to safety from the flames that appeared to envelope him, cheers for his victory too.'
**Albert Moody**

Children, meanwhile, were finding that war added new dimensions to their lives:–

'We youngsters searched the streets for shrapnel, often heard rattling down the roofs of our houses. The shrapnel came from the anti-aircraft shells. With other boys, I would swap pieces of my collection; sometimes I was favoured by a choice piece, such as a part of a nose cap.'
**Hugh Turpin**

'My little sister and I now slept in the "big" bed with Mother. There were booms from "our Gun" as we crouched – what fun! – under the kitchen table hung about with blankets . . . '
**Louise Eickhoff**

Mary Jay remembers that the anti-aircraft gun on the hill by Whitestone Pond was nicknamed the "Pale Blue Gun" by local children because of the colour of its paint.

The response of many adults to the bombing was to flee London for places of greater safety. Few adults could have contemplated the air raids with the equanimity displayed by the gentleman who wrote this letter to a local newspaper:–

'Sir – Taking the area of London as one hundred square miles; taking a circle of sixty yards in diameter with oneself at the centre as the area within which, if a bomb fell, one would be seriously inconvenienced, and assuming that the enemy succeeds in dropping 22 bombs in London every month all the year round; assuming also that there is an equal likelihood of a bomb dropping at any one point as at any other, the war will have to last thirty-two years for it to be likely that a bomb will fall within one's own circle. In other words, in thirty-two years of such bombing there would be an even chance for and against such an event happening. Again, the chances would be against a direct hit on one's roof of ten yards square if warfare of this intensity were to continue for **894** years.
If people realized such facts as these there would be no more panic.'
**Hampstead Advertiser,** 21 February 1918, p7

*West Hampstead

11

# CHAPTER FOUR

# SAVINGS AND SEMOLINA

Britain had been at war for over two years before a Food Controller was appointed (in December 1916) and a Ministry of Food established "to promote economy and to maintain the food supply of the country". By 1917 the full menace of submarine warfare to shipping and hence food supplies was becoming only too apparent.

Sugar was the first article to be rationed. Britain's supply came from abroad, and according to Mrs. C.S. Peel (in "How We Lived Then, 1914-18". Bodley Head, 1929), nearly seventy per cent of our pre-war consumption was beet sugar from Germany and Austria.

Milk was the first dietary item to be controlled and sugar the first for which ration cards were issued. Early in 1918 it became impossible in London and the Home Counties to buy butter, meat or margarine without ration cards. The allowance was usually 1½ lbs. of meat per person per week for adults and 10 ozs. for children under 10. Each person was also allowed 4 ozs. of butter or margarine and 8 ozs. of sugar. By the end of April 1918 nationwide meat rationing was in force.

Louise Eickhoff remembers how, as a child at this time, she enjoyed prodding molten tar streaks in the road to make her fingers smell delicious:–

'. . . and Mother would have to squander her precious butter (reserved for those with children when it was available in Heath's the Grocers*) to clean our hands "fit for little ladies". Margarine not only had a horrible taste but was less efficacious as a tar-remover.'
**Louise Eickhoff**

Infringements of the Food Control regulations by traders led to frequent prosecutions. The following are two typical cases reported in the **Hampstead and Highgate Express** of 19 May 1917:–

'At the Marylebone Police Court yesterday (Friday) week, Edith Fleming, an assistant at the shop of John Sainsbury, provision merchant, Queen's Crescent, was fined £3, or twenty-one days imprisonment, for . . . a most distinct infringement of the order of the Food Controller by refusing to sell sugar, unless tea, coffee or cocoa was also bought. Mrs Anderson, of 75 Haverstock-hill, said that the defendant was weighing up sugar when she entered the shop, and having purchased some margarine she asked for ½lb. of sugar. The defendant replied, "I cannot let you have sugar

*Bernard William Heath, grocer, 48 Flask Walk, Hampstead.

**18** Children or invalid's milk priority card, 1917/18

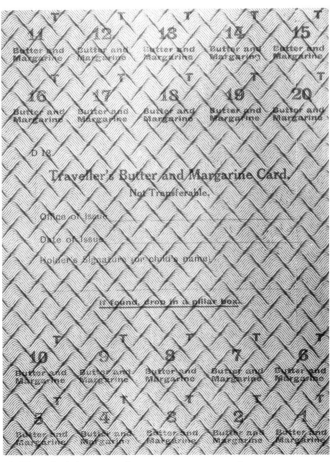

**19** Traveller's butter and margarine ration card

**20** The Home and Colonial Stores, 253 Kentish Town Road, mentioned in the news item. (Photograph dated 3 January 1904)

## THE PEOPLE'S KITCHEN,

### 10 NETHERWOOD STREET.

Open Daily (except Sundays), from 12 to 2 p.m.

### WHY SHOULD I GO THERE ?

**Because** of economy of food and fuel to win the war.

**Because** co-operative buying and cooking economises food and fuel.

**Because** regular customers and more of them means cheaper buying.

Therefore you help your country
you help your neighbours
and you help yourself
by helping the Kitchen.

| SERVED HOT DAILY. | |
|---|---|
| Soup, Potatoes, Greens, etc. | 1d. |
| Milk Pudding | 1½d. |
| Fruit Pudding and Tarts | 2d. |
| Sausage Rolls, Cornish Pasties, Rissoles, etc. | 3d. |
| Meat Dishes, Stews, Pies, Puddings, etc. | 4d. |

Meals to be taken home, not eaten at the kitchen, so bring your own covered dishes, cans, baskets, etc.

Support the Kitchen now, you will want it more in the winter.

Its success is in your hands; The Committee will do their part, if you do yours.

**21** Poster advertising the People's Kitchen, 10 Netherwood Street, Hampstead, opened in September 1917

unless you buy either tea, coffee or cocoa." The witness asked, "Don't you know that that is against the law?", and to that the defendant replied, "We must protect ourselves, or we should not have enough to go round for the regular customers." The manager of the shop afterwards served her, but remarked that if some restriction was not imposed they would sell nothing but sugar, and would not have enough to go round.

The defendant denied that she imposed any condition, and said her instructions were not to do so. She only had two half-pounds of sugar in the shop, one of which would have been given to the customer at the time had she waited.'

'At Marylebone on Tuesday, Edith May Jenkins, manageress of the Home and Colonial Stores, 253 Kentish Town Road, was fined 20s. for imposing a condition when selling sugar that tea must be purchased.'
**Hampstead and Highgate Express,** 19 May 1917, p6

The local newspapers of this period are full of advice about food and fuel economies. People were encouraged to grow their own vegetables, and substitutes for scarce food items were recommended. These included the use of glucose in marmalade-making, and of soaked tapioca as a binding agent instead of eggs.

The **Hampstead Advertiser** patriotically expounded the virtues of "War" flour, though with a cautionary note:–

'Good, wholesome and appetising pastry may be made with "War" flour, but it is unwise to attempt most of the various kinds of puff pastry. Plain short pastry gives the most satisfactory results.'
**Hampstead Advertiser,** 29 March 1917, p7

"War" bread had become general on 1st January 1917:–

'War bread has a little deeper colour than the ordinary bread, but is as sweet, palatable, and as nourishing, if not more so, than the loaf to which the public are accustomed.'
**Hampstead Advertiser,** 4 January 1917, p8

Various ingredients went into "War" bread, including rice, maize, oatmeal, beans and barley.

By 1917 potato stocks were dwindling and mangold wurzels and swedes were being strongly recommended as substitutes. According to the **Hampstead Advertiser:–**

'Experiments at the Food Control Offices show that they are, properly treated, very palatable,'

and gave the following recipe:–

1 lb. mangold wurzel
¼ lb. vegetable butter/dripping
2 small onions
Pepper and salt
'Cook the mangold wurzel in the butter for about 20 minutes, or until tender. Then add the onion (which has been previously chopped), and pepper and salt. Drain for a moment before serving on cooked lentils, buttered rice or cheese sauce.'
**Hampstead Advertiser,** 12 April 1917, p7

Food economy was taken very seriously. The **Hampstead Advertiser** of 11 January 1917 announced a visit by the Pudding Lady to the Wesleyan Chapel Hall, Lisburne Road, to speak on wartime housekeeping. In the course of an hour and a half, she cooked dinners as well as dispensing household hints. The cooked food was then sold at the end of the meeting.

In furtherance of the food and fuel economies, the "People's Kitchen", 10 Netherwood Street, "conveniently situated in a poor working-class neighbourhood", was opened in September 1917, as part of the Hampstead Food Control Campaign. It was not a charity, but a co-operative undertaking and the prices charged were intended only to cover the costs. If it ran at a loss, it was to be closed down.

# FUEL ECONOMY

## Some Simple Hints

It is patriotic to use Gas instead of coal for cooking—but to use it otherwise than economically is waste—so learn to use your Gas Cooker economically.

Don't boil a quart of water when you only need a pint. Don't let your pans boil over—turn down the gas directly the contents boil.

When you're going to use the oven, get it thoroughly hot first—then put in as many dishes as possible. After a quarter of an hour or so, turn down the oven burners—you'll spoil the food and waste gas if you don't.

Turn out the gas the moment you've finished cooking—you'll save a useful sum of money in the year.

*"How to Use a Gas Cooker" is a helpful handbook which will be sent post free on application to the Gas Light & Coke Co., Horseferry Road, Westminster, S.W.1*

T.371.

**22** Fuel economy advertisement in the **Hampstead Advertiser** of 19 July 1917, p8

---

# The Tank is Coming,

## ST. PANCRAS MUST BE TO THE FORE!

### Buy! Buy! Buy!

## War Bonds & 15s. 6d. Certificates

from

☞ **THE TANK** ☜

which will be at

## The Cobden Statue, Camden Town,

On Wednesday & Thursday, March 6th & 7th.

Open for Business from 9 a.m. to 9 p.m.

### BACK YOUR SAILORS & SOLDIERS WITH YOUR MONEY.

---

**23** Advertisement for St. Pancras Tank Day in the **Hampstead and Highgate Express** of 2 March 1918

Tickets were purchased at the entrance to the Kitchen and then exchanged for food, which was carried away in the purchaser's own receptacles. So successful was this venture that just over a week after opening the Kitchen was serving between 300-400 customers every weekday from 12-2 p.m.

The fear of some food items becoming unobtainable often led to hoarding:–

'Mrs. Henrietta Lewy, of West End-lane, Hampstead was summoned at Marylebone for hoarding food. An inspector of the Ministry of Food said the quantities of food found at defendant's house were: 46¾ lb. of tea, 15 lb. sugar, 30 lb. syrup, 42 lb. of flour, 18 lb. coffee, and 16 lb. flaked rice. Fines and costs amounting to £10 were imposed.'
**Hampstead Advertiser,** 14 February 1918, p2

Fuel also posed problems. Coal shortages gave rise to accusations of coal hoarding in private cellars and provided ample opportunities for profiteering. Prices rose alarmingly, and the London County Council found it necessary to introduce a bye-law by which coalmen had to display on their vehicle a metal tablet. On this there was to be clearly marked in a permanent way, the price per cwt. of coal. Hitherto, as the **Hampstead Record** noted:–

'. . . the carmen had been able to chalk the price up and rub it out or alter it at their own sweet will.'
**Hampstead Record,** 12 May 1916, p6

One of the local newspapers records an amusing incident in connection with this:–

'A trolley coalman in Somers Town on Saturday was considerably perturbed by a sudden rush for his coal. In five minutes he had received orders for about five times the quantity his trolley held. Exclaiming to the large number of excited women surrounding him, "Don't all speak at once," he climbed on to the trolley and then discovered the reason for the demand.
The price of the coal as shown by the tin tickets stood at 1s 1d instead of 1s 11d per cwt. One of the figure "1's" had fallen down, that was all, but the women of the neighbourhood were under the impression that the millenium had arrived, or that the war was over.'
**Hampstead Record,** 10 November 1916, p5

During the winter of 1917/18 the coal ration was as follows: 2 cwt. for 3-5 rooms, 4 cwt. for 6-7 rooms, and 8 cwt. for dwellings with over 12 rooms. The summer rate was half the winter rate and some extra was allowed for invalids, young children and lodgers.

**24** Hampstead's civic dignitaries with Sir Gerald Du Maurier the actor-manager (second from right) outside Finchley Road Station on Hampstead Tank Day, 4 March 1918

**25** Advertisement for Hampstead Tank Day in the **Hampstead and Highgate Express** of 2 March 1918

**26** Albert Zwanziger's baker's shop at 385 Kentish Town Road – one of those shops with a Germanic name in jeopardy during the anti-German riots. (Photograph dated 10 September 1904)

Newspapers also encouraged more unusual forms of economy:–

'Instead of selling old bicycle tyres for a few pence, use them for soling your boots . . . an expert . . . can get at least six pairs of soles and heels out of the old discarded cycle outer cover, and each pair wears, according to quality, from one to two months.'
**Hampstead Advertiser,** 18 January 1917, p7

As well as economising in food and fuel, war savings were another way in which those at home could feel they were contributing to the war effort. Up and down the country, tanks such as "Nelson" which stood in Finchley Road on Hampstead Tank Day, were used to boost the War Savings Campaign. As John Walter, who saw one in Fitzroy Square, surmised, they were also used to boost morale.

War Bonds were available, as were War Savings Certificates for those only able to save smaller amounts. St. Pancras had the novel idea of holding a raffle for the buyers of bonds and certificates, the person with the winning ticket receiving a money prize.

### Anti-German feeling

Perhaps inevitably many Germans settled in this country suffered hostility and discrimination during the war. Nationalist paranoia was prevalent, as Louise Eickhoff recalls:–

'Mother had to go to the Police Station: very puzzling for we knew she was not a naughty person. But some folk (local paranoia attributed it to THEM in the Buildings in Flask Walk) had seen smoke coming out of our chimney in a strange fashion; and as we had a German name and our father had disappeared, the police needed reassurance that Mother was not signalling to him on the Enemy side!'
**Lousie Eickhoff**

John Walter vividly recollects what it felt like to belong to the family of an enemy alien:–

'Because our father was German and had not been naturalized he was interned soon after war broke out leaving our mother with five young children . . . We moved in with "uncle" Hans who occupied the whole house above his hairdresser's shop at number 20 (Warren Street). We had to leave our comfortable home at Kensal Rise, Willesden, where we were all born because we could not afford the rent there any more. "Uncle" Hans Hochheimer was also a German but he had been naturalized and was therefore not interned. However, this did not save him from having his shop windows broken after it had somehow got around that he was a German . . .
Times were very hard for our mother who had to find work to keep us all reasonably fed. Being the wife of a German internee this was not easy as she was discriminated against by some officials. Her first job was at an officers' hospital in or near Fitzroy Square, this was menial and badly paid. Later she found work in an aircraft factory near where now stands the State Cinema, Kilburn. . . It had not been easy for our mother to get taken on for this better paid work. She succeeded, may-be, because her two younger sisters were already employed there.
Discrimination by some authorities was still a worry which only changed after our mother's brother, uncle Tom, an army captain on leave from France went in full uniform to enquire about the reasons for the bad treatment our family was receiving. From then onwards things became better.'
**John Walter**

Resentment against German shopkeepers sometimes found expression in letters to the local newspapers, like this one from a gentleman in West Hampstead:–

'Sir – There are numerous shops in West Hampstead – as also in other parts of Hampstead – run by Germans: one of these, a Baker's, is open *all day on Sunday,* while all British-owned shops are closed. Why is this permitted? Without wishing to advocate the violence of other quarters of London, I certainly think that all householders in this locality should be patriotic enough to boycott these shops. I am told that a dinner was actually given in West Hampstead to "celebrate" the sinking of the Lusitania, and I also know that a similar convivial meeting was held elsewhere in Hampstead "in honour of the punishment" of Scarborough!*
How long is this insolence to be endured?'
**Hampstead Advertiser,** 13 May 1915, p7

*Scarborough suffered a German naval bombardment on 16 December 1914.

Feelings ran high with the sinking of the "Lusitania" on 7 May 1915 and a few days later there were attacks on German bakers' shops in Kentish Town. On the night of Tuesday 12/Wednesday 13 May some damage was done in Malden Road and Queen's Crescent, but police threw a cordon round the threatened neighbourhood thereby frustrating further trouble. However, on the Wednesday morning, shop fronts were smashed while police attention was diverted and bread and cakes were looted.

A baker's shop in Mansfield Road and a barber's in Fleet Road were also wrecked. According to the **Hampstead and Highgate Express** of 15 May 1915, p6, from which this report is drawn, "thousands of women and children took part in the rioting, but there were not many men in the crowd".

Many people with Germanic-sounding surnames, from the Royal Family downwards, found it prudent to either change or anglicise these names. This happened in Camden as elsewhere; the 1913/14 Camden and Kentish Towns directory lists a Mrs. Rose Konig, baker, at 265 Kentish Town Road. The 1922 directory lists a Mrs. Rose *King,* baker, at the same address.

CHAPTER FIVE

# ARMISTICE

'Perhaps my clearest memory of World War I is the moment of its ending. My sister and I were at St. Margaret's School, Oak Hill Park, at the time. As we all assembled in the hall when the Armistice was announced on November 11 1918, two of the mistresses sank down on a sofa, holding hands and gasping, speechless with relief. I can see their faces still and remember their names to this day.'
**Mary Jay**

'They *knew* the Armistice was coming at New End School. How could they when there was no radio? . . . but they did. There was an unusual restlessness after the day's start, and teachers debated whether to send the children home . . . But we had to be released: our mothers had come in a body with flags to wave and cheer with on the way home; all except mine who had had no money to spare. How deprived I felt! It was like magic that mothers should know that the War was over and produce flags from nowhere.'
**Louise Eickhoff**

In London there was wild rejoicing in the streets at news of the Armistice, but even those who took part in the festivities remarked on the pain beneath the revelry. Even during the celebrations news was still coming in of those killed just before the ceasefire.

For the lucky ones, life returned to something approaching normality. Louise Eickhoff's father returned safely from the war, and after his demobilisation, she writes that:–

'Just suddenly things were as before, the music, the shared early breakfast, walks to the Park and the Band . . . and the comfort of the murmur of a man and woman's voices and sound of piano playing under our beds in the darkened room at night.'
**Louise Eickhoff**

John Walter's father went straight to Germany from internment when the war ended, "believing that chances of work for him as a German would be very slim here in England". His family followed soon after. (Some of them returned to England after Hitler's rise to power; John Walter was a member of the Holborn Civil Defence team during World War Two).

Others, like William Carson and Edwin Prosser, never returned at all.

CHAPTER SIX

# WE MUST BE SAFE

When it became clear that Britain could once again be involved in a major war the London boroughs began a campaign of enrolment in the Civil Defence Services. Residents were able to use their particular abilities and training in the various voluntary services.

During the war years the A.R.P. wardens became familiar faces in their districts. Their first duty was to report incidents but they were also at hand to give advice and help.

The post of Air Raid Warden could be dangerous as this incident, on 1 November 1940, illustrates:–

'Eton Place was lucky in having a large tree which caught up the parachute, swung the bomb which ended up in a large coke heap with its detonators pointing skywards. Hearing a thump, one of our gallant air raid wardens stepped outside to investigate and was caught across the throat by a mysterious rope. He felt his way along it, in the darkness, until he felt a large metal object as big as he was and, correctly deduced, unfriendly. All tenants were roused and given a few moments to evacuate the block. The bomb was later defused and we were lucky.'
**Alan Yates**

**A.R.P. ST. PANCRAS ENROL MUST BE SAFE NOW**

**27** St. Pancras A.R.P. (Air Raid Precautions) recruitment poster.

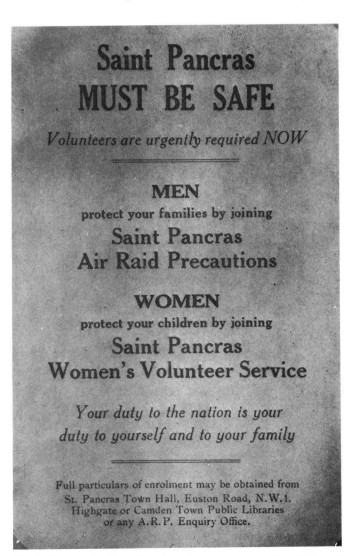

**28** St. Pancras leaflet calling for volunteers to join the A.R.P. and W.V.S.

**METROPOLITAN BOROUGH OF SAINT PANCRAS**

*Air Raid Precautions Department*

**ENROLMENT FORM.**

Name (IN BLOCK CAPITALS) _____ Mr. Mrs. Miss.

Address (Business) _____ Address (Private) _____

Telephone (Business) _____ Telephone (Private) _____

Age _____ Occupation _____

Are you a British Subject? _____ Have you a driving licence? _____

Are you able to provide a car? _____

Service which it is desired to enter _____

| WOMEN. | MEN & YOUTHS. |
|---|---|
| Air Raid Wardens. | Air Raid Wardens. |
| First Aid Posts. | First Aid Parties. |
| Ambulance Drivers and Attendants. | First Aid Posts. |
| Report Centres and Communications. | Rescue and Demolition Parties. |
| Miscellaneous Duties. | Report Centres and Communications. |
| Drivers for Wardens Posts. | Miscellaneous Duties. |
| | Drivers for Wardens Posts. |

NOTE:—Volunteers for service in First Aid Branches of A.R.P. work are requested to complete "A" below if they already hold a certificate of First Aid Training and "B" below if no such certificate is held.

"A" I wish to offer my voluntary services as a member of the First Aid Personnel enrolled under the St. Pancras Air Raid Precautions Scheme.
I will make every effort to attend such classes for post instructional training as may be arranged.
_____ (Signature).

"B" I wish to attend a course of First Aid Lectures and undertake on completion to sit for the examination necessary to obtain the First Aid Certificate, either of the British Red Cross Society or of the St. John Ambulance Brigade.
As soon as I have obtained this certificate, I wish to be considered a Volunteer for service as a member of the First Aid Personnel under the Saint Pancras Air Raid Precautions Scheme.
I will make every effort to attend such classes for post instructional training as may be arranged.
_____ (Signature).

Have you any knowledge of Anti-Gas, First Aid or Nursing? (give particulars) _____

Please give details of any other qualifications or knowledge which you think may be useful _____

Days most suitable for attending lectures _____ Afternoon or evening _____

[P.T.O.

**FOR OFFICE USE ONLY.**

| M/L Classification _____ | Index No. _____ |
| Acknowledged _____ | Group Area _____ |
| | Course No. _____ |
| | Certificate No. _____ |

**29** St. Pancras A.R.P. enrolment form

**30** Photograph showing the Chief Warden of Hampstead A.R.P., Lieutenant Colonel J. Rowbottom, D.S.O., M.C., the Assistant Chief Warden, Dudley Hassan and the five District Wardens

**31** Photograph showing Auxiliary Fire Service fire fighting equipment taken from the window of Bolton House, Frognal Rise, Hampstead

A knowledge of the locality could be invaluable.

'I had volunteered to serve in the police war reserve when an appeal had been made early in 1939 and had attended lectures at Rosslyn Hill Police Station. When the warning sounded on Sunday September 3rd following the Prime Minister Neville Chamberlain's radio speech I had already been sworn in at Rosslyn Hill. For the next few weeks I spent much of my time directing aliens living in Hampstead to the police station to register. Many of them had fled from the Nazi persecutions and now had to face internment in a country they had begun to think of as home.

Night duty at Rosslyn Hill often meant patrolling a beat covering the Lawn Road Hospital, St. Stephen's Church and the Playhouse Cinema. A small area but should a bomb drop in the vicinity it could involve many casualties. Or you could find yourself patrolling the entire Heath. If you would like to try this out in the daytime – start at Whitestone Pond, proceed at a leisurely pace along the Spaniards Rd. cut through the Highgate end of Kenwood into Millfield Lane down to Highgate Rd. (Swains Lane) where you would normally phone the station. Cross the path at the foot of Parliament Hill, then either cross the footbridge and proceed towards Agincourt Rd. or carry on toward Nassington Rd. From there you would make your way to East Heath Rd. and Rosslyn Hill. Some Hendon College Cadets had been attached to the station when the College closed down and were assigned to the Heath beat at first but after one fell in a pond and another had got lost, the Heath was left to those of us who knew the area. As one who had spent his life so far in the area I was one of the obvious choices.

Patrolling the Heath round the ponds on a moonlight night in the small hours of the morning in the winter is no recommendation for police work. Among our duties we were expected to see if anyone had committed suicide by throwing themselves into the ponds or hanging themselves on a tree. Shadows can play some nasty tricks with your imagination – believe me.'
**E.G. Halse**

Many people served the community as Fire Guards in the A.R.P., as members of the Auxiliary Fire Service or simply by keeping watch at night for fires started by incendiary bombs.

'My moment of reverie was brought to a sudden end by a piercing schwishing sound as incendiaries fell all around. The thought of being alone was also dispelled as people milled around, all intent upon dousing these new destructive weapons of war. All were successfully dealt with, even some which fell on a roof in Prince of Wales Road – the only roof to suffer but that only slight because we were able to get to the roof so quickly – providence decreed that a builder's ladder should be left raised on the front of this property. What a frightening experience this was, despite the training most of us had had, you don't realise you are afraid until afterwards, that's a good job too isn't it.'
**Albert Moody**

'1938 saw the enrolment of many volunteers for training as Wardens, Firemen, Ambulance Drivers – men and women alike. My work in the building trade and my use of ropes and ladders made me a "natural" for the Fire Service, hence my training and passing out as an Auxiliary Fireman long before September 1939. I wasn't very pleased when, on the outbreak of war, I was told to resign from the A.F.S. and hand in my uniform, building operatives being reserved for rescue, demolition and construction of buildings. It was because of this that I was in the darkened Harmood Street when all those fire bombs fell. What a good job I had had fireman training.'
**Albert Moody**

**32** Two members of the A.F.S. with a sub-officer of the London Fire Brigade at Bolton House

**33 34** Hampstead Home Guard on parade

The Local Defence Volunteers or Home Guard was formed from local volunteers. They were never called upon to fight but learned to defend their homes in other ways.

'The Home Guard did many good jobs during the war, reservoirs and many other installations coming under their wing, not to mention the manning of anti-aircraft sites, which brings me to the East Heath Road where a dozen or so of the Holmes Rd. lads were sent to make up the strength of the "Z" Battery Anti-Aircraft who were stationed on the site there. The site was manned in the daytime by the "regulars" and at night by the Home Guards, during air raids both were on duty, the regulars manning Bofors Guns – H.G. manning rocket projectors. The Home Guard made up three troops of gunners, one as the engaging troop who occupied a Nissen hut on site to be first at hand when the warning went, the two other troops who were billeted in a house in Well Walk. Thirty men to a troop and when the warning lights went up in the billet there was such a rush to get down to the site, the noise created must have woken up half of Hampstead.'
**Albert Moody**

Members of the Territorial Army were also making preparations for the defence of London.

'Guilford Street, between Holborn and St. Pancras, at noon on the 3rd September, 1939: an hour earlier, the United Kingdom had declared war on Germany. The sirens stirred in the still autumn air, slid upwards and wailed, London's first wartime air raid warning. The tension of waiting for war was over. My diary on the previous day recorded ". . . we have delivered an ultimatum to Germany to leave Polish territory or we fight. She replied: 'We are not at war. We are merely rectifying frontiers.' " Disbelief that the worst could occur, desperate optimism, was shattered by the sirens.

That sound caught me on sentry duty at the gates of Coram's Fields as a sapper, one of a detachment of a Territorial Army Searchlight Company of the Royal Engineers which I had joined seven months earlier. From the railings of this childrens' playground, one looked across Guilford Street to Guilford Place at the top of Lamb's Conduit Street. There a drinking fountain under a worn stone statue of a girl with a water jug decorates a tiny roundabout which isolates the public lavatories beneath the road. I watched a policeman direct a solitary, bemused civilian to shelter, probably in Russell Square Station, and proceed on his beat: then the streets were deserted.

Before the sirens' moan subsided our little Irish lorry driver – generator operator ran out of the adjoining Boy Scout H.Q. to put a gas-cape round my shoulders and, as I thanked him, scurried back inside. Bombs, possibly with gas, could be expected to fall in the immediate vicinity within the hour, it seemed. I thought of the sentry in Pompeii whose body, preserved in cold lava, was found, centuries later, in the ruins: a brave idiot, to obey the call of duty against instinct?

Twenty minutes passed. No aircraft had been heard, no rumble of bombs or gunfire. A plane coming up the Thames estuary, it was reported, had proved to be "one of ours". The all-clear sirens rising to an unwavering chord, came as an anti-climax, awoke slumbering butterflies.

For our emplacements, we filled sandbags outside the Foundling Hospital's offices and child care centre, built only a few years before to the north of Brunswick Square. We shared a mound of sand, tipped into a corner of the roadway, with relays of civilians filling bags for their own purposes. Evacuees, fearful and tearful children from the locality, assembled there on one of these days to be transported away from their homes and families. There was little comfort in the name tabs and labels strung round the necks of the children or the gas-masks in cardboard boxes slung over their shoulders. How long does it take to recover from the sensation of such misery?

When not bagging, we wielded pick and shovel to dig holes, for our equipment and for a dug-out command post, in the rubble of the playground, incidentally uncovering some of the vaulted cellars of the Foundling Hospital. At night we manned the searchlight and practised the operating drills, with aural locating equipment, replaced a few years later by radar but then quite adequate to guide a searchlight beam onto bombers whose top speed was little over 120 m.p.h. However, no enemy plane came over London that winter. Occasionally we saw distant beams focused on a target, invisible to us, while we stood around shivering in the exposed cage, waiting for "air co-operation" if not for action, to give us night practice.

We were on a three minute alert every third night. Until a hut was built where we had first slept in tents, we would doze on the wooden benches in the open-fronted summer house with the pretty green copper roof, still there in the middle of Coram's Fields, the gift of a Viscount Rothermere to commemorate the death of two sons in World War I. Our Section Officer – at one time 2nd Lieutenant Widgery, years later Lord Chief Justice of England – would arrive unpredictably in the small hours to turn us out, from what passed for sleep in our boots and, practically, in our wide-brimmed helmets, to action stations inside the wire, within three minutes: but that was "just testing".

**35** Hampstead Home Guard outside the Belsize Avenue entrance of the old Hampstead Town Hall

**36** Holborn Civil Defence Rescue Services at work

On the four hour night watches one of the sentries would guard the lorry, just inside the gates, warming up the engine regularly on cold nights – and occasionally being caught asleep in the cab. Another would patrol like a caged animal inside the wire fence, a perimeter of about a quarter of a mile and the third would hover near the dug-out (most of it over-ground) close to the "blower", a direct telephone line to an anti-aircraft operations room. They were hours mostly for dreaming, asleep or awake.

Early in the New Year, 1940, there was heavy snow. At 0530 hours on a Sunday morning in January our Officer Commanding came to call us out. We had been expecting him for hours, tipped off by others earlier on his round, so there was little credit in our being the only detachment out of fourteen to turn out that night in under three minutes. But the Major kept us standing in the snow for a pep talk: our cold and weary discomfort over-shadowed the intended encouragement. We got more pep from our regular call-out comforter – a billycan of steaming hot tea so strong and sweet that it might have been cocoa. Within a week of this incident, however, torrential rain transformed the snow into lakes of slush across the surface of the playground. Then we were relieved at Coram's Fields and dumped miles away in an open field in Mill Hill.

After that (though not necessarily in consequence) Camden had its share of the bombs that fell on London. On the night of the 8th/9th September 1940, Coram's Fields was hit and evacuated as a searchlight site, and many old buildings in the vicinity of Theobalds Road were destroyed in the following months. The detachment was dispersed as the phoney war – and playing soldiers – ended.'
**Michael Rubinstein**

When the bombing started, Elizabeth Sadler was able to put her nursing experience to good use. After working for a time as a shelter nurse she was transferred to a First Aid Post in the evacuated St. Margaret's Hospital, Kentish Town. She describes life at the post during a lull in enemy action:–

'Inside the sand-bagged entrance was the perpetual darkness of the black-out, with stone corridors lit by the dim light of 25 watt bulbs, leading to the main mess-room and heart of the post. Here there were bright lights and gaiety abounded. Here the spirit of the "Blitz days" was fanned and kept alive, along with an attitude of "mustn't let old Hitler get us down". And after 7 p.m. the best antidote to "old Hitler" seemed to be a non-stop round of social activities such as whist drives, dart matches and general knowledge quizzes. Sometimes there were lectures by a visiting Medical Officer or First Aid and bandaging classes and having bound or trussed each other into varying positions, those who had done the bandaging would go off to prepare the late night cup of cocoa leaving their victims to unravel themselves as best they could. About this time black beetles would appear and scuttle around the floor and send the more nervous females leaping on to chairs to avoid them. By midnight, if all was quiet, we would drift off to our respective camp beds and putting our shoes out of reach of the black beetles, roll up in grey blankets for the last of the twenty four hours of our rota.'
**Elizabeth Sadler**

This relatively peaceful existence disappeared when long-range rockets began to fall on London.

'At the First Aid Post the decks were cleared for action and all card-tables and dart-board swept out of sight. In the office the phone rang day and night "Air Raid Warning Red" and "Air Raid Warning White" and the staff were primed and ready too. No more nights of loosened corsets and slipped-off shoes, rolled in a blanket on a camp bed. Now firmly corseted and shod, all of us did a hard twenty four hours on duty. When not out, we sat "on call" through bright summer days and nights – they seemed the same under the electric light – not even noticing the black beetles now; but listening to the distant vibrations and distant thuds. And one of the stretcher-bearers would say "That's not ours – too far away". adding sadly "Some poor devil's had it." '
**Elizabeth Sadler**

**37** Members of Holborn Civil Defence Rescue Services lowering
the injured from an upper storey

'I remember a hot sultry day in early July when we were called out in the Mobile Unit to an incident at Dartmouth Park Gardens on the borders of Islington. We drew up beside what had once been a row of houses. Three were in ruins and a choking pall of plaster-dust lay over everything mixed with a sickly sweet smell of escaping gas. The Light and Heavy Rescue men were clambering over the rubble, forming a team and passing down the debris of doors, windows and joists as they began their search for trapped casualties. We began to treat minor casualties who had crawled out of the adjacent houses, for cuts, gashes and shock. Some were quite unhurt, just people with blackened lips and dust grey hair whose eyes shone bright with excited relief at finding themselves alive. Another flying-bomb came over, obscenely spluttering and hardly a soul glanced up as it flew over. Then a Rescue man held up his hand for complete silence and everyone listened. Was that a muffled tapping or a faint, buried cry? The frenzy of activity continued and presently casualties were found. They were put on a stretcher and the doctor knelt down to attend to them. Some were taken to the ambulances; some the doctor signalled to be taken away. Covered by A.R.P. blankets, the bodies were left beside a wall across the road. Soon there were more of these blanketed shapes to be laid in neat rows and counted. Later a girl was found trapped on a staircase with half a house balanced on a broken bannister across her back. A red "M" for morphia was painted on her forehead and for hours the Rescue Parties worked to free her, tempering their strength with the delicacy of surgeons as they eased the great mass of masonry from the strut of wood that supported it and at last brought her out alive.'
**Elizabeth Sadler**

'My war took place, not in "Camden" but in Holborn, then the smallest and for its size the richest of the London boroughs. My war service was spent as a part-time ambulance driver in the L.C.C.'s London Auxiliary Ambulance Service, the L.A.A.S. (known to us in disillusioned moments as the Lousy Amateur A.S.). Really we were very effective and our Station 55A, in the garage under the Coram Street corner of Russell Court, must have saved many lives. We part-timers however, were at the end of the queue when calls came and I must admit that we sometimes secretly longed for the prolongation of an incident so that we could see some action.

As in all services, life on duty alternated between periods of intense boredom broken by short bouts of frenzied activity. We developed the usual feeling of superiority to those not in the uniformed services, referring to them as "civilians". In fact nothing could have been more civilian than the L.A.A.S, whose personnel was made up of people thrown out of work by the war, others waiting to be called up, general misfits and a few do-gooders like us part-timers.

We were derisive about press colour stories on our activities, which often referred to us as "Mercy Girls", though actually the sexes were mixed, so that periods of boredom could be made bearable, not only by endless games of pontoon, but also by short-lived and frequently reshuffled romances.

Our ambulances were mass produced white wooden boxes, mounted on, for the most part, Ford chassis and closed at the rear by canvas curtains, although at first any kind of delivery van was pressed into service and for some time I drove about labelled "Kemp's Biscuits". Because of my lowly status as a part-timer I did not carry out a great number of missions, though I remember the bomb which fell in the middle of Russell Square and blasted a "colonial" students' hostel on the north side so that the curly hair of the African students we picked up was full of tiny slivers of shattered glass, very difficult to extract.'
**Judith Todd**

CHAPTER SEVEN

# STAYING ALIVE

Finding a safe place to sleep for the night was a constant worry. Not all homes were suitable for the provision of private shelters. The local authorities provided a number of surface and deep shelters for the public.

'As we lived in a flat above our business, there was nowhere to put a shelter. Hampstead tube station was too far to walk with one's bedding at night (in any case, all available space was very quickly snapped up) and there were no other deep tubes nearby. Fortunately, the authorities had put up a road shelter for daytime raids on the pavement outside us and opposite the old Hampstead Public Library, then in Finchley/Arkwright Road. Although narrow, damp and noisy (it was continually being shaken by passing traffic), sleeping there was preferable to being killed in one's bed. We struck up acquaintanceships with the people in the big houses across Finchley Road as well as those living in the flats above nearby shops. We were all equals under the bomb.'
**Mary Elsy**

Some people had other solutions:–

'We had no shelter at home, as we were on the middle floor again at Eresby Road but put a frame of a big double bed on the kitchen floor with a large deal table over it. We slept there, mum and dad and I during the Blitz, though sometimes, if no warning had gone before we went to bed but had sounded in the night, I found myself, the next morning, standing up in the built-in cupboard, surrounded by clothes, where I had been put for "safety".'
**Jean Haynes**

**38** Shelterers in Holborn Station

**39 40** Refreshment arrangements in Holborn Station

'We were in the thick of the bombing. Time bombs caused us to evacuate our homes – one almost penetrated into the cellar of the Prince of Wales pub, its nose just poking through the front wall. Another came to rest under the kitchen floor of a house lower down the street where a man was sleeping off a drinking session of the night before, he was sleeping under the kitchen table and it didn't wake him up. Sleeping arrangements were made for us in the school hall down the street but my wife and I preferred the open air to being buried in bricks and mortar so we opted for good old Hampstead Heath. The first night we spent in the open but afterwards went to a surface shelter on Spaniards Road. We were walking across the Heath one evening and had just passed the Vale of Health when an almighty explosion threw us onto our faces, we must have triggered off a time bomb buried in the mud. We got to our feet filthy but fit and proceeded on our way. A lady warden who had charge of surface shelters in that area was at "our" shelter when we arrived and we reported this to her for the sake of the records.

We had some small measure of rest having taken a mattress to lie on after the first night. Our "exile" lasted ten days and when, after being home a couple of days, the lady warden of "our" shelter came to our shop for cigarettes she nearly had a fit to see my wife who she believed had, with me, been killed by a direct hit on our shelter. A tramp who had used the shelter was found but not finding us they assumed us blown to bits!! So many times we escaped death or injury, we just knew we had a Guardian Angel protecting us.'
**Albert Moody**

The obvious place of refuge for Londoners was the nearest underground railway station. Life in communal shelters had its disadvantages.

'As air raids became nastier and more frequent, people one knew had narrow escapes. It was becoming dangerous to sleep in one's own bed at night. I used the Northern Line from Hampstead tube station to St. Pancras. Now, not only were the trains crowded, but the platforms too as people dumped themselves down to sleep on the hard stone. Bunk beds were only later provided by the authorities. To avoid the appalling smell which built up over night in the tube, I took to cycling from Hampstead through Regents Park to St. Pancras.'
**Mary Elsy**

'I had been advised after a short illness to give up full-time hospital nursing and find something less strenuous so I joined the St. Pancras Civil Defence for the remainder of the war. At first I had tried to find gainful employment in Hampstead Civil Defence, but just then there had been a brief lull in enemy action and they had no vacancies for me. To begin with I helped staff the Medical Aid Posts in Underground stations and other shelters in the Borough. For a while I was sent to a shelter under the Coach Station at King's Cross. I remember there were large pipes running along the walls at ceiling level and above the camp bed where I sometimes rested. These pipes were warm and at quiet moments around 4 a.m. big rats would creep along them doing a sort of trapeze act above me; while below I grew pale with suspense as to whether or not they'd make it or land on my head.
When there were no "incidents" to cause a rush, shelter nursing was a fairly routine job. Mostly doling out Brompton cough lozenges or aspirins for headaches, looking for spotty-faced children with infectious rashes and dealing with minor complaints. The doctor visited us at 10.30; there was tea, then a check on the drug-cupboard and look at anyone who needed the doctor's attention. Later when the pubs were all closed things began to get lively. The shelter marshals struggled valiantly with drunks, settled squabbles among the shelterers and kept a lookout for verminous or dirty bedding.'
**Elizabeth Sadler**

**41** The occupants of Swiss Cottage Station settle down for the night

**43** Sketch by Olga Lehman of a concert in Carkers Lane Shelter, 25 January 1941

Gradually it became clear that people were not to be dissuaded from sleeping in the stations. The local councils tried to make life a little more comfortable for the shelterers. Bunks were installed, toilets provided and refreshments made available. Previously, people sleeping in Swiss Cottage Station had to travel by train to Finchley Road Station to find a proper toilet!

Sometimes entertainment was brought to the shelters which helped to pass the long hours underground.

'Cinemas and theatres generally kept to matinee performances but in Goldington Street, St. Pancras, Unity Theatre continued and I was one of the volunteers on the lighting staff. We were anxious to take entertainment to those unable to come to the theatre and I recall being attached one evening to Alfie Bass and Bill Owen for an expedition to amuse the unfortunates crowded on the tube platform. My job was to carry a spotlight, plug it in somewhere down below and to introduce the "cast", not so well known then as they are now. Their efforts were much appreciated.'
**Alan Yates**

# The Swiss Cottager

## De Profundis

**Organ of the Air Raid Shelterers at Swiss Cottage Station**
**London, N.W.3**

### BULLETIN No. 2

WE HOPE that our first issue was well-received by all Swiss Cottagers. It has earned wider notice, too, and "The Times," "The Daily Telegraph" (which also had a photograph of it) and "The Daily Express" all praised it. That was very gratifying, for we need all the publicity we can obtain in order to make Tube-shelterers as comfortable as possible.

\* \* \*

PENDING the Government's decision on the question of deep-shelters, there is a growing opinion that, as a short-term policy (for, after all, something needs to be done *immediately*) the installation of three-tier bunks on tube platforms would be hailed with relief by the thousands of people who nightly use the tube-station platforms as dormitories, and by the thousands more who, because of lack of space, are prevented from doing so.

\* \* \*

THE ADVANTAGES of this are manifold.

Primarily, they would increase the accommodation and so enable more people to have rest and slumber, to say nothing of safety.

They would occupy no more—indeed, less—platform space than is now taken up nightly.

Conditions would be less dangerous to health.

It would more easily enable the station platforms to be kept clean.

They would mean that thousands of Londoners would be enabled to escape the cold and damp of surface-shelters in winter-time.

There would be far less difficulty over the question of reserving places on the platforms. Very likely the problem would no longer exist, for it is conceivable that local users of tube-station shelters might be able to have their regular bunks. There would be equality of comfort for the shelterers.

And the task of the Committee, the station-staff, and the police would be rendered so much easier.

MEANWHILE we are aware of complaints regarding people who reserve places for groups hours before darkness falls and would be very pleased to check this practice, which is unfair to those whose work prevents them from arriving until dusk. But the problem is a difficult one, the more so since any person has the right to enter any tube station as long as it is open. Any practical suggestion will be welcomed and, if possible, acted upon.

Users of deck chairs make our task more difficult, and it is possible that in future they will find themselves stopped by authority from entering the station with them. The Committee's primary aim is *to provide as many sleeping places as possible*. You may be uncomfortable where you lie, but it is blue-pencil more uncomfortable to have to walk about all night for lack of a place to sleep in.

\* \* \*

WITH LITTER you are still being far too generous. PLEASE leave the station in the condition in which you find it. It takes but a few seconds for you, but it takes an hour or two of the station-staff's time to make the place presentable most mornings. So will you take your wastepaper, wrappings, cartons, paper-bags, etc., away with you?

\* \* \*

WATER is now being carried round nightly by the stewards. Please bring your own cups.

\* \* \*

TEA: We are seeking facilities from the Board to make tea for you. Thus you could be assured of having it nightly, at an early hour.

P.T.O.

# CHAPTER EIGHT

# THE TERRIBLE COST

The southern part of the present Borough of Camden was hardest hit by enemy action. In the tiny borough of Holborn about one seventh of its property was destroyed and 426 people died as a result of the air raids. 621 were injured badly enough to be taken to hospital.

'Mere figures cannot convey the terrors of the heaviest attacks, they cannot reproduce the scene when Theobalds Road area was burning, and they cannot do justice to the courage and fortitude of the citizens of the borough, whether in helping in the civil defence work during those fearful nights or in carrying on their ordinary occupations during the respite of the days.'
**Holborn Official Guide 1956**

**45** The west side of Gray's Inn Square after the incendiary attack on 12 May 1941

**44** Lamb's Conduit Street from Theobalds Road after an incendiary attack on 12 May 1941

**46** Bomb damage to the area north of Theobalds Road. The photograph was taken from the Liverpool Victoria Building in Southampton Row. Streets shown are, Old Gloucester Street, Boswell Street and New North Street

London Transport had its share of problems, both above and below ground.

**49** Damage to Drummond Street after an incident in November 1940. The blast damaged the Underground tunnel beneath the road

**47 48** Two photographs of St. Pancras Station after the air raid 10 May 1941 when five bombs fell on the Station

Air raid casualties for the Borough of St. Pancras have been estimated at 957 killed and 1,443 injured and taken to hospital. The raid of 10/11 May 1941 was exceptionally severe. On that night 52 high explosives, 1 parachute mine, 9 unexploded bombs and hundreds of incendiary bombs landed in the Borough. C. Allen Newbery, the Chief Warden of St. Pancras recalls that fires were so numerous that the Fire Brigade could not deal with half of them. Fire Guard parties, fire-watchers and householders gallantly tackled many by themselves.

However, this terrible night signalled the end of the Blitz on London and there were no more air raids in St. Pancras until October 1943.

The area around St. Pancras and King's Cross Stations was an obvious target for enemy bombers. It was one of the major railway centres of London, with an electricity generating station and gas-works close by.

Both stations were badly damaged during the war. St. Pancras Station was closed for five days in the autumn of 1940 when three incidents occurred within the space of one month but the most serious damage was caused on the night of 10 May 1940. One high explosive bomb fell through platforms three and four and exploded in the vault below.

**50** Damage to Camden Town Station

Even Underground stations were not completely safe. For example, in one incident in October 1940 a number of people were killed in Camden Town Station.

**51** Parachute mine damage in Fellows Road, 1941

Although Hampstead had no military objectives worthy of aerial attack and no great railway termini like St. Pancras, it nevertheless suffered its share of the bombing. In the Borough 204 people were killed and 383 were injured badly enough to be taken to hospital.

West Hampstead with its concentration of railway lines attracted a large number of bombs but few areas of Hampstead escaped unscathed. Like the rest of London Hampstead fared badly on the night of 16/17 April 1941. A parachute mine fell in Fellows Road, completely destroying six houses, killing 24 people and injuring many more.

Hampstead was more fortunate during the big raid of 10/11 May 1941, when 13 high explosive bombs fell in the borough but by great good luck they all failed to explode. In the last phase of the war, when conventional bombing was replaced by pilotless aircraft and rockets, 10 "flying bombs" fell in Hampstead, helping to make Broadhurst Gardens the most bomb-damaged road in the borough.

**52** The old Hampstead Central Library in Finchley Road after a high explosive bomb destroyed the Reference Library in 1941. The building was used as a Warden's Post, and the blast killed a lady warden. The building is now the Camden Arts Centre

Some Hampstead residents remember lucky escapes:–

'Alas, I suppose it had to happen to us in the end. But we were lucky! Early that fateful night, before a bomb labelled "Finchley Road" was due to fall, some old friends who lived in Edgware called in on my mother and kindly whisked us back to their home for a good night's sleep. We received the news at breakfast time. "Our bomb" had fallen directly on the Public Library, killing the personnel of an A.R.P. post there and blowing off the head of a passing cyclist. The street shelter had fortunately stood firm although the people inside had been badly shocked. The entire front of Langfiers Court Photographers had been blown in and the rooms behind wrecked.

I went to work as usual (one always did if one could on these occasions: it was partly defiance to the Germans, partly one's own small contribution to the war effort), but I was allowed to return home early. I found my mother walking among the debris, wringing her hands. "What's to become of us" she moaned.'
**Mary Elsy**

June 1944 saw the start of a new form of aerial attack – pilotless aircraft. Six months previously, Civil Defence services had been warned to expect some form of attack like this, and Control Room staff had been trained to receive the message, P.A.C. (Pilotless Air Craft). These became better known as V1s or flying bombs.

Camden resident Mary Jay describes how the British public first became acquainted with this weapon:–

'The public had no idea what was happening when the Flying Bomb assault began and at first the authorities did not know much more. Cautious daily statements were broadcast: "There was some enemy activity over southern England . . .

some damage was caused and there were casualties". The first of these new weapons – referred to variously as Flying Bombs, Fly Bombs, V1s, or later sarcastically as "Doodlebugs" – fell on June 12 (1944). On the morning of June 15th, we woke to a fresh type of horror. The air raid warning, which we had hardly heard during the last two years, began sounding every fifteen minutes, followed closely by the All Clear. I normally travelled to work by the North London overground line from Hampstead Heath to Willesden Junction. That day, as we filed out of the station, handing in our tickets, people were asking each other whatever it was all about. "It's the invasion", declared the ticket collector, "troops landing every fifteen minutes". Was he joking? I could not tell and hurried on to work. There, one of the surgeons walked into the office and said: "My view is they're pilotless planes". How right he was. The Doodlebugs flew so high that, on the rare occasions when you saw them, all you saw was a small black spot surprisingly high up for the roaring it created; then, when its giro stopped, in preparation for the dive earthwards (the "cut out") there was silence until it reached the ground and exploded. I saw one of these black spots high in the sky one morning from the platform of Hampstead Heath Station. From the nature of the roaring, one might have thought it was right upon us. But no, it was almost invisible and landed far away. There was something quite eerie about these monsters whirling on a set course with nobody in them. Indeed, our own pilots were said to find them more unnerving than the piloted planes of the enemy. This reaction was eloquently expressed in a dialogue between two women overheard discussing it. One asked the other whether she found the bombers of the first Blitz or the Flying Bombs the more unpleasant. The other replied: "O, I'd rather the piloted ones: they did 'ave that 'uman touch".'
**Mary Jay**

**53** In May 1945 one of the last rockets to fall on London landed near the Hampstead Central Library, Finchley Road, damaging the building for the second time

A flying bomb provided Sarah Reeks with her worst experience of the war:–

'On Saturday November 25th 1944 a fly bomb fell in Oppidans Road at 5 a.m. killing many people. The owner of one of the houses in which people lost their lives had asked us some years beforehand if mother and I would like to move into it, we declined. Had we gone to Oppidans Road we would have lost our lives. November 25th was the worst experience we had throughout the war. We were in the front semi-basement room and slept with the heads of the beds against the passage wall. The dog slept underneath the armchair in the corner facing the room door. When the bomb fell, the windows were shattered, the room door blew in and plaster from the wall came on to our beds. We groped our way into the back room, unaware that we had walked over the door. When it was light and we could view the damage done, we saw our beds covered with plaster which had fallen from the wall and the only clear spaces were where our heads had been resting.'
**Sarah Reeks**

One resident remembers well the day she and her husband decided to forsake the Anderson shelter in their garden for the safety of Hampstead Underground Station:–

'We heard the planes coming over each night. On 18th September I decided I felt unsafe and must go deeper and prepared to go to Hampstead Tube as it was the deepest. My husband was in the first gas attack in 1915 at Ypres and he still felt the effects of it with occasional sickness etc. and I felt I should not expose him to more bombing merely to let me be in the garden shelter. After 7 o'clock we set off walking up

Frognal in a glorious sunshine promising a typical Heath sunset. We had only gone down to the platform by the time the bombers arrived. There were quite a few hundred people already crowding the platform. After spending a restless strange night we came down Frognal at about 6 a.m. and saw West Hampstead Green was shrouded in a thick grey powder. Mill Lane which we must walk along was roped off and the Warden stopped us and when we said " . . . but we *live* in Holmdale Road at no. 35" he answered "There ain't no 35" and so it was when we finally turned into Holmdale Road we saw the great hole and gap in the houses, 4 gone, 5 people killed and many injured. A team of men were digging to find us and neighbours could only say that we slept in the shelter each night. It was now very full of rubble – the alarm clock was still ticking. The men found the base of the 500 lb bomb which was about where our bed had been. We have it now – a gruesome reminder of what war is.'
**Isabel Hay**

Others were not so fortunate, like one A.F.S. telephonist:–

'This brave young lady, on duty at her post in Mansfield Road School, tracked a flying bomb all the way across London from South to North, its course in direct line with her post. She knew it was overhead, but stayed put – the beastly thing "cut out" and blew her and the post to pieces.'
**Albert Moody**

The rockets, or V2s as they were known, were a rather different proposition: no warning was given and nothing seen or heard until it exploded on impact, the explosive in the rocket's warhead producing a deep crater and total devastation close by. Some people, however, preferred these to the flying bombs, on the principle that there was not time to get anxious; after the explosion, one was either alive or dead!

The same air of mystery surrounded the arrival of the V2s, as has been noted with the V1s:–

'Again, no one knew what was happening at the start, and the first few sudden crashes came without warning of their approach; though, if they fell very near, it was possible to hear the swish through the air as they dived to the ground. Attempts were made to avoid alarm and despondency by cautious reports that these weird bangs denoted "burst gas mains". And so they were popularly described until we knew what they really were: long-range rockets launched from the French coast. Later we learnt that these rockets were tubular weapons forty-five feet in length and containing about one ton of explosive. It is believed that London may have survived only because they were few and late and vastly expensive to produce, so that most of their launching sites were put out of action by the advancing Allied armies.'
**Mary Jay**

Terrible as they were, the early bombing raids provided a morbidly fascinating experience, as several Camden residents remember:–

'I remember one episode of great excitement when walking to a friend's in North End Road at night. There was an air raid going on and the Highgate bus had been abandoned at the War Memorial. Everyone had presumably fled into the Jack Straw's Inn for comfort. The sky was ablaze with beauty, caused mainly by searchlights, like a great celebration. I climbed into the bus, and the metaphysics of that half hour in my life are with me still. For a while the world belonged only to me, and because of my youth it seemed a wonderful experience.'
**Hazel Riches**

'It was an exciting time. One was part, even if only an insignificant one, of a giant drama being played out all around. I well remember the night when a crowd of us from the street rushed up on to the roof of our house, (it was a flat one, on which we had played as children), to watch a 20th-century version of the great fire of London, an epic, a breath-taking event. City buildings and sky were lit by towering flames. Searchlights, thin paths of light, crisscrossed the surrounding darkness. We ignored the screaming bombs, the droning planes, the crashing gunfire. It was too magnificent a sight to be missed. One hoped that no-one was being hurt, although common sense told one that they must be. One prayed egotistically that the falling bombs would find their way on to neighbouring houses, rather than one's own.'
**Mary Elsy**

# CHAPTER NINE

# MAKING DO

Food rationing was introduced gradually, bacon, ham, sugar and butter being the first rationed items in January 1940. In March, meat and in July tea, cooking fats and margarine were added to the list. Other items followed later, including cheese. Offal was excluded from the meat rationing and fish was unrationed but hard to find.

On 1st December 1941 the points rationing scheme came into operation. Every holder of a ration book received sixteen points a month, later raised to twenty, to spend as he or she wished at any shop that had the required items. At first, only canned meat, fish and vegetables were on "points" but in the following year, many more items were added, including condensed milk, breakfast cereals and biscuits.

During the Second World War rationing appears to have been more systematic and to have worked better than that of the First World War. It also had one unlooked-for but beneficial result; the British people were far healthier in 1945 than they had been in 1939!

One Camden resident had first hand experience of the administration involved in food rationing:–

'That first "proper" job, found through the Labour Exchange was in what is now Camden's Town Hall. It was then known as St. Pancras Town Hall. St. Pancras's local food office had been set up in its theatre on the ground floor. I was allocated to the counterfoils department. Every British citizen had been given a ration book. They chose their retailers, who filled in the appropriate counterfoils. These registrations were dispatched to the local food office, where they were kept in rubber bands and filed away in drawers. As people were continually coming and going, registering and cancelling, these counterfoils, filed alphabetically under shops, were continually being taken out, recounted, some removed, some added. This was my job, exquisitely boring but fortunately discipline was not very strict and I remember this period as being a cheerful and giggly one.'
**Mary Elsy**

Some shopkeepers were not over-scrupulous about the provisions they sold to their customers and where meat was concerned most people were desperate enough to buy almost anything. Not always however:–

**54** Painting by Grace Golden of the Emergency Food Office in St. Pancras Town Hall.

'We were registered for meat at a butcher's in Regents Park Road. One Saturday I went for the meat and asked for two small chops which were with others on the counter. He said "You cannot have chops they have been ordered, you can have this breast of mutton." I did not like the look of it but having no choice I had to buy it. On Sunday when the meat was in the oven, I did not like the smell. Mother and I tried a small piece and could not eat it. On Monday morning I took it to the butcher and told him the meat was bad. He ate a small piece and said "Nothing wrong with it." I told him he had better keep it and let me have two chops. He refused. So I went to the Town Hall and asked to see the Health Inspector. He was sympathetic and said "Leave it with me." Later that day the inspector arrived at our house with two chops. The butcher had to replace the bad meat.'
**Sarah Reeks**

Restaurants did their best with the food available to them, sometimes with highly successful results:–

'When I started work at the factory, eating was quite a problem but I soon solved it.

After I arrived home in the evenings, I was much too tired to cope with so much as boiling an egg, so lunch was a necessity. We had an hour's break for this and, after sampling the works canteen on the first day, I went in search of something more gastronomically acceptable and soon found it, only a few yards away, at Antolini's Cosy Café.
Joe Antolini was a gaunt, six-foot-plus Italian, married to an enchanting five-foot-nothing Cockney. Before he set up his own small business he had been a chef at the Ritz. Needless to say, he did the cooking and his wife looked after the customers. He produced wonderful meals with the small amount of rationed food he was allowed and she went on shopping forays to Soho, returning laden with such unrationed treats as brains, sweetbreads and tripe. I was certainly their most favoured client. They knew exactly when I would arrive and how long I would stay. My small table was always reserved. I never had any idea what I was going to eat, knowing only that I would enjoy it and my meal always ended with a cup of freshly ground black coffee.'
**Caroline Ramsden**

'Until we were comfortably installed in the Scout H.Q. we ate in an excellent workmen's dining room or an Italian cafe at our end of Lamb's Conduit Street; we were given army meal vouchers for our meals but not for beer, consumed generally at The Lamb across the road, packed and smokey. If we were keen to study the seamy life associated with dubious little hotels we went to The Cross Keys on the site now occupied by the Theobalds Road Post Office. We could expect only four or five hours broken sleep most nights. Those who indulged in a beery night-cap were especially hard to rouse for sentry duty at 0400 hours.'
**Michael Rubinstein**

Food rationing was undoubtedly a burden and any alleviatory measures were gratefully received.

'A house in Nutley Terrace was taken over by the W.V.S. and opened daily for lunch, a wonderful happening for food was a real problem, or should I say lack of it. The dishes were without protein of course, made from dried eggs, vegetables and potatoes but how grateful I was; with only one ration book life was indeed hard. A lot of people knew someone who knew someone and how I envied them. My employer went without nothing – he knew a butcher in Kilburn High Road and every weekend he collected his meat for himself and his wife, large joints which were but a dream to the rest of us.'
**Hazel Riches**

Despite the difficulties, some traditions were maintained.

55   Harvest Festival at the bombed St. Bartholomew's Church, Gray's Inn Road, October 1942

The shortage of meat was irksome but people were encouraged to compensate for this and also to make their dinners more nourishing by adding oatmeal or dried pulses. "Ration Dinners" published by the Central Council for Health Education was a pamphlet with several suggestions for meatless dinners such as:–

Pea, vegetable and milk soup. Hard brown bread. Steamed fruit pudding.
**or**
Parsnip, carrot and potato pie, gravy, greens. Bottled plum pulp and custard. Glass of milk.

The local authorities realised how important it was to keep up the morale of the people who stayed at home, dodging the bombs and making the best of their food rations. War Savings Weeks and special funds were set up, primarily to encourage people to put money into National Savings Certificates and War Bonds but also to give them an opportunity to help the war effort themselves by contributing towards extra equipment for the armed forces.

## HAMPSTEAD WAR WEAPONS WEEK
### May 17th—24th

Complete this form and send it to your Banker now.

To.................................................Bank, Ltd.,
.................................................Branch

*Dear Sirs,*

*Please purchase on my/our behalf and debit to my/our account accordingly:—*

£.....:............ 3 *per cent. Savings Bonds,* 1955-65. *(No limit.)*

£.................... 2½ *per cent. National War Bonds,* 1946-48. *(No limit.)*

£.................... 3 *per cent. Defence Bonds.* (Maximum holding, £1,000.)

My Bond Book No. is.................

£.................... *National Savings Certificates.*
(Maximum holding, 500 units. £375.)

My Holder's No. is...................

**Please arrange for the above sum to be included in the Borough of HAMPSTEAD'S total for War Weapons Week.**

Date...................                    Signature...............................

Address  ...............................

...............................

56   Application form for War Savings Certificates and War Bonds in aid of Hampstead War Weapons Week

**57** A tank outside Finchley Road Station used to promote War Weapons Week in Hampstead

**58** Holborn War Weapons Week Parade passing Holborn Town Hall in High Holborn, May 1941

**60** The Hampstead Hurricane

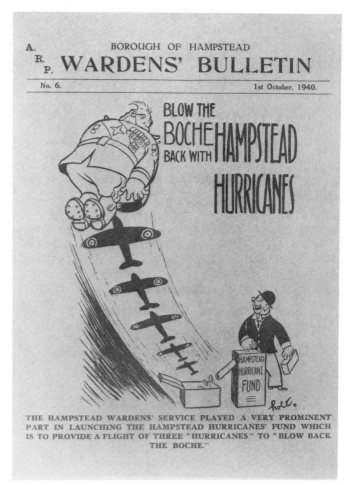

**59** Cartoon which appeared on the cover of an issue of the Hampstead Wardens' Bulletin. The Hampstead Hurricane Fund was set up under the presidency of the Mayor of Hampstead to collect funds for the provision of a flight of three aircraft from the people of Hampstead

The St. Pancras Travelling Library was opened by the Mayor of St. Pancras, Alderman Evan Evans, J.P., on Saturday 8 February 1941. In his opening speech he declared:–

**'We are going to deliver food for the mind to the doors of the people . . . Books, libraries, education, knowledge, culture and learning are all the enemies of dictatorship and the foundation of freedom, liberty, and self-restraint. Books will strengthen us to beat Hitler.'**

This innovatory mobile library meant that books could now reach people using billets, rest centres and A.R.P. shelters, as well as those unable to get to their usual library because of the Blitz or war work. It also formed part of a borough-wide scheme to encourage reading, which already included the highly successful opening of libraries on Sundays.

The local newspapers reported the Travelling Library's first call:–

**"On Monday morning at The Grove, Highgate Village, the library's first port of call, car-loads of stretcher parties and rescue men from a nearby depot had arrived to take advantage of the new service. "It's just the thing we need for A.R.P.", said a burly stretcher bearer to an "Express" reporter. "It's rather awkward to get at a good selection of books, and all we get given to us at the depot are magazines and girls' books."**
**Hampstead and Highgate Express, 14 February 1941, p3**

The Travelling Library proved not only a great success but a media attraction. Over forty newspapers and periodicals reported the opening ceremony, and British Movietone News included a feature in their newsreel.

The Library stopped at twelve central points in the borough for three hours at a time, and from 29 June 1942 the library hours were extended for the summer to cover 6.30-9 p.m.

The service was finally discontinued on 15 September 1945, and the library van was returned to Hastings.

62 The Mayor of St. Pancras, Alderman Evan Evans, opening the travelling library in 1941. He is holding the first book borrowed; a volume of Winston Churchill's speeches

61 The St. Pancras Travelling Library was the first of its kind in London. The vehicle was hired from Hastings Borough Council

---

CHAPTER TEN

# THE DAY PEACE BROKE OUT

V.E. Day (the end of the war in Europe) was celebrated on 8 May 1945, with bonfires, parties and revelry in the streets. For one Labour Councillor in Holborn, the war ended like this:–

'My last recollection of life as a Councillor is also my last recollection of the war in Europe. On V.E. Day, protocol required that the Mayor, accompanied by Aldermen and Councillors, should read from the Town Hall balcony a proclamation of the cessation of hostilities. The Holborn Town Hall, the balcony of which looks on to what was then an inconsequential part of High Holborn was ignored by most of the traffic, which by-passed it in favour of a two-way New Oxford Street. We assembled accordingly shortly before 11 a.m., when the Mace Bearer handed out long blue councillors' robes which we had never seen before. Suitably robed, we proceeded to the balcony, where the Mayor read the proclamation and we stood round him graciously smiling and ready to receive the applause of enthusiastic crowds.

Unfortunately these were reduced, by the obscurity of the situation and the greater attraction of the Mall and Trafalgar Square, to a handful of councillors' friends and relations, three schoolchildren with a dog and two Canadian soldiers seated on the kerb and celebrating victory in an independent way out of a bottle. So, with a faint ripple of applause, ended my war in Camden.'
**Judith Todd**

# ILLUSTRATIONS

## WORLD WAR ONE

**1** Recruiting advertisement, 5 September 1914.
**2** Artists Rifles sentry on the Lancing Street Schools.
**3** Artists Rifles headquarters, Duke's Road.
**4** Royal Engineers Signal Service in training on Hampstead Heath – an advance lookout party, January 1915.
**5** Men of the Queen Victoria Rifles, 9th London Regiment seen during training near Whitestone Pond, Hampstead, January 1915.
**6** Official letter notifying his wife of the death of Gunner Edwin Prosser of wounds received in action, November 1918.
**7** Rosslyn Lodge Auxiliary Hospital, Lyndhurst Road, Hampstead.
**8** Patients in one of the wards at Rosslyn Lodge Auxiliary Hospital.
**9** The Artists Rifles V.A.D. Hospital, Lyndhurst Road, Hampstead.
**10** The Artists Rifles V.A.D. Hospital. Patients knitting.
**11** Advertisement for the Hampstead War Hospital Supply Depot, 7 April 1917.
**12** War Hospital Supply Depot staff engaged in producing hospital supplies.
**13** Leaflet printed by Hampstead Council of Social Welfare advising people on what to do during an air raid.
**14** Air raid damage to the German Gymnasium, Pancras Road, King's Cross, during a daylight aeroplane raid, 7 July 1917.
**15** The St. Pancras Hotel after the aeroplane raid of 17/18 February 1918.
**16** The result of an air raid on Gray's Inn, 13/14 October 1915.
**17** Damage to the Bedford Hotel, Southampton Row, caused by an aeroplane raid of 24 September 1917.
**18** Child's or invalid's milk priority card, 1917/18.
**19** Traveller's butter and margarine ration card.
**20** The Home and Colonial Stores, 253 Kentish Town Road, 3 January 1904.
**21** Poster advertising the People's Kitchen, 10 Netherwood Street, Hampstead, opened in September 1917.
**22** Fuel economy advertisement, 19 July 1917.
**23** Advertisement for St. Pancras Tank Day, 2 March 1918.
**24** Hampstead's civic dignitaries with Sir Gerald Du Maurier outside Finchley Road Station on Hampstead Tank Day, 4 March 1918.
**25** Advertisement for Hampstead Tank Day, 2 March 1918.
**26** Albert Zwanziger's baker's shop at 385 Kentish Town Road, 10 September 1904.

## WORLD WAR TWO

**27** St. Pancras A.R.P. (Air Raid Precautions) recruitment poster.
**28** St. Pancras leaflet calling for volunteers to join the A.R.P. and W.V.S.
**29** St. Pancras A.R.P. enrolment form.
**30** The Chief Warden of Hampstead A.R.P., the Assistant Chief Warden and the five District Wardens.
**31** Photograph of Auxiliary Fire Service fire fighting equipment taken from the window of Bolton House, Frognal Rise, Hampstead.
**32** Two members of the A.F.S. with a sub-officer of the London Fire Brigade at Bolton House.
**33** Hampstead Home Guard on parade.
**34** Hampstead Home Guard on parade.
**35** Hampstead Home Guard outside the Belsize Avenue entrance of the old Hampstead Town Hall.

**36** Holborn Civil Defence Rescue Services at work.
**37** Members of Holborn Civil Defence Services lowering the injured from an upper storey.
**38** Shelterers in Holborn Station.
**39** Refreshment arrangements in Holborn Station.
**40** Refreshment arrangements in Holborn Station.
**41** The occupants of Swiss Cottage Station settle down for the night.
**42** The Swiss Cottager.
**43** Sketch by Olga Lehman of a concert in Carker's Lane Shelter, 25 January 1941.
**44** Lamb's Conduit Street from Theobalds Road after an incendiary attack on 12 May 1941.
**45** The west side of Gray's Inn Square after the incendiary attack on 12 May 1941.
**46** Bomb damage to the area north of Theobalds Road.
**47** St. Pancras Station after the air raid of 10 May 1941.
**48** St. Pancras Station after the air raid of 10 May 1941.
**49** Damage to Drummond Street after an incident in November 1940.
**50** Damage to Camden Town Station.
**51** Parachute mine damage in Fellows Road, 1941.
**52** The old Hampstead Central Library in Finchley Road after a high explosive bomb destroyed the Reference Libary in 1941.
**53** Damage to Hampstead Central Library, May 1945.
**54** Painting by Grace Golden of the Emergency Food Office in St. Pancras Town Hall.
**55** Harvest Festival at the bombed St. Bartholomew's Church, Gray's Inn Road, October 1942.
**56** Application form for War Savings Certificates and War Bonds in aid of Hampstead War Weapons Week.
**57** A tank outside Finchley Road Station used to promote War Weapons Week in Hampstead.
**58** Holborn War Weapons Week Parade passing Holborn Town Hall in High Holborn, May 1941.
**59** Cartoon which appeared on the cover of an issue of the Hampstead Wardens' Bulletin. The Hampstead Hurricane.
**60** The Hampstead Hurricane.
**61** The St. Pancras Travelling Library.
**62** The Mayor of St. Pancras, Alderman Evan Evans, opening the Travelling Library in 1941.

## ILLUSTRATION SOURCES

The illustrations used in this publication come from the Camden Local History Library's collection with the exception of the following:–

**Nos. 38, 39, 40, 41, 49, 50**
London Transport Photograph Library
**Nos. 4, 5, 14, 15, 16, 17**
Imperial War Museum
**Nos. 1, 11, 23, 25**
"Hampstead and Highgate Express"
**Nos. 7, 8**
British Red Cross Society
**Nos. 31, 32**
Miss V. Black
**No. 54**
Grace Golden